A La
A Lamb

"Poetries of God's inspiration"

Mischka Reid

ISBN: 9781713348351

DEDICATION

This book is dedicated to every soul who is hurting, broken, in need of some emotional support and spiritual healing. May your souls find rest in God and may these few words put a smile on your face. The world is filled with critiques, hypocrites and backbiters, but may this be an uplifting book to you that you may find peace and be the change that the world needs. The world needs love.

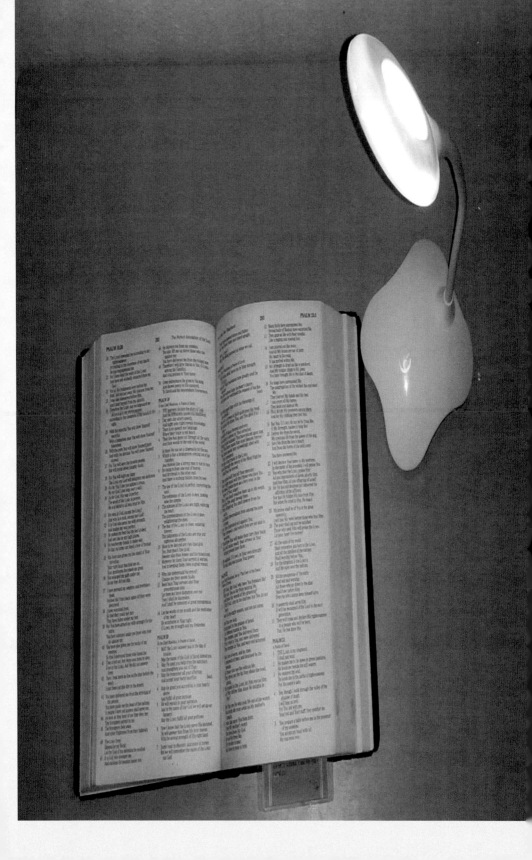

CONTENTS

ACKNOWLEDGMENTS

Let me first thank the Holy Spirit who is the Divine Comforter. Without Him I would not have been able to find peace nor have the insights given to write these few master pieces. I thank everyone who has encouraged me to write poems and who has supported me emotionally. Cheers to Errica Burgher who was the main person who forced this talent out of me, to Shanice Jones who is a real cheerleader and to Briton Marrett (a.k.a my best friend); and lastly, a big thank you to Zavier Cheverriah who took the time out to proof read this document.. You have all made it possible and so I share with you my gratitude.

POEM OF ENCOURAGEMENT

Oh boy, back to school again
Where mommy, daddy and the whole family will spend.
It is a stressful time but no worries my dear,
Remember! God is always near.

Off to school you go where you'll be on your own
Just know that Jesus is with you so you're never alone
In this Christian race you may grow tired, want to give up and become insecure,
Keep in mind the word of God, "the race is not for the swift, but for those who can endure".

You will be in a different environment with many temptations
And you will encounter many spirits that will try to break your concentration.
Fast and pray, and let there be praises in air
We are not wrestling against flesh…, this is a spiritual warfare.

The devil will entice you to go against your faith
Take it from me brethren, don't take the bait.
Put on the whole armor as encouraged by Paul
That you may withstand the evil one who will try to cause you to fall.

You are all very important in God's eyes
Be strong in the Lord and please be wise.
Because you represent Christ the devil will always be in your way
No need to fear, Jesus is and will be fighting your battles every day.

Peace Be With You.

FUN FACT!

The previous poem was written at a time when college students were about to head back to university. At this point I didn't even know I could write poems in full. I suppose I should thank Errica Gooden-Burgher her practically forced me to exercise my talent of writing poems. She discovered this when every post card I would give to someone had a stanza where the sentences ended in rhymes ☺

2018 IN REVIEW

New year greetings I bring
As I look back on the past and the fact that I am still living…
…I give God praise for my well-being!

The path was rough as there were a few obstacles in the way
But praises be to Jesus who led me each day
Many tears were shed when I felt burdened to travel this Christian road
Then Jesus said, "child be of good cheer and give Me your load".

There were many times in 2018 when I felt lowly at heart
Because everything felt like it was failing right from the start
But Jesus assured me saying, "because you're not seeing a clear path doesn't mean you have failed!
Keep trying, a successful saint is one who through trials and temptations has always prevailed."

2018 was filled with trials and faith testings
But there were also continuous seasons of blessings
This was my testimony of the year 2018 in a short review
The following stanza is now my message to you…

To live to see 2019 is another chance to repent of your mess
Stop playing around with God and start giving Him your best!
Christ died on the cross so we could reign with Him
Please don't let 2019 be another year of meddling in sin!

"Jesus Christ the same yesterday, today, and forever" (Hebrews 13:8)
Jesus Christ is Lord all year round.

FUN FACT!

I remember sitting down in my living room doing this poem (the "year in review"). I didn't make it to watch night service and so I had decided to use my time to do something constructive for the Lord. I urge you the reader to challenge yourself to a "be still" moment when all you do is sit and LISTEN to what God has to say to you; perhaps He wants to reveal to you a/some hidden talent(s); perhaps He wants to increase your anointing in some area of the sort…listen, there is no telling what God wants to do with you, but the fact that you are here means you have a lot of purpose and you are important. Please, do not waste your life focusing on the wrong things. You have one life to live, live it wisely!

I WILL STILL LOVE YOU

I will still love you,
Not just for today but for our whole lives through,
In and out of season…
A love so pure and unconditional I won't have an objective or reason.

I will still love you,
Even when you test me and I don't know what to do,
Even if our fights start an eruption,
We've gotta work it out because divorce is not an option.

I will still love you,
80 years from now when we are still going strong and learning things anew,
We'll grow weary physically as the years pass by,
But my love for you shall never fail nor die.

I will still love you,
When I'm old and senseless and haven't a clue,
Even up until my last breath,
I'll love you till death.

So you see, my love is still,
I only pray for us God's perfect will,
May we be all that God wants us to be,
Though throughout all of this, will YOU still love me??

FUN FACT!

This one was obviously written for a wedding haha! But whose wedding? Who was I inspired by? Well congrats to the Burghers!!! Hoooooraaaaay!

DARLING, KEEP STANDING ON THE WORD

Have you ever felt dismayed
Because you made so many plans and not one prevailed?
Darling, Keep Standing On The Word

Have you ever felt cursed
Like God has forgotten you while putting everybody else first?
Darling, Keep Standing On The Word

There was a time I wanted to die
I questioned my existence and asked God, why?
He said: "Darling, Keep Standing On The Word"

Then I became envious of my enemies who prospered and lived like
the Fresh Prince of Bellaire,
And I thought to myself, 'God is really unfair!!!'
With a smile, still He said: "Darling, Keep Standing On The Word"

You know, I understand what I am saying,
Because before I knew God, the only thing I was excelling at was
failing;
But then I understood God's word in Jeremiah 29:11
And I experienced and embraced that peace that could only come from
Heaven
All because I Kept Standing On The Word!

You see in the end it is not about you and the world
There is One who will judge you according to the standard of His
Word
So Darling, Keep Standing On The Word!

You can never go wrong if you do…

FUN FACT!

Here we go again, being asked to write yet another poem according to the theme of that day's service at church. The theme was "The Word", or something like that. Who remembers everything in perfect order??? Thanks to the Holy Spirit who inspires to write. Trust me, prayer fixes everything! As a matter of fact, it is said that prayer is the bridge between panic and peace ☺ While we are meditating on that, I'd like to say that this poem is dedicated to my family. Many of them are not yet saved, but I am praying and standing on the word of God.

HAPPY BIRTHDAY

Sometimes things go wrong and don't go the way you want
But because you've tried many times and failed doesn't mean you can't
You wear a broken smile and others think you're alright
But only you and God know your fight.

You try to be strong even though you feel weak
Not once did you complain
You ought to be commended because you're meek
Your task isn't easy, you have to deal with people who are obscene
But regardless, you're admired
Because you display the love mentioned in 1 Corinthians 13.

Happy birthday sweet pea
You mean the world to everyone, including me
Never back down, attack each challenge
With Christ all things are possible and I know you can manage.

Many people lose their way living up to other people's expectations
And when they fail they suffer condemnations
Don't be like them, well it's just my thought
Stay true to who you are, and continue being that rarest jewel that can
never be bought.

FUN FACT!

This poem was written exactly for the occasion presumed, a birthday. I especially love the last stanza and I take great pleasure in dedicating it to some strong women who I admire a lot. Kenene, Psalmonie, Shanice, this is for you with love!

GOD IS LOVE

Some men asked, "how do you know there's a God?"
He wields all this power in His hands yet He allows very few good
compared to the bad!
The intensity of our pain and problems are high with no help from
above…
And yet you say that God is love!

My response to these broken hearts,
Was nothing short of the wisdom and knowledge that God imparts;
My friends you know God was with us from the very beginning,
And He's still with us even though we chose a life of sinning.

Though humans can be callous and more often than not obscene,
Christ's perfect love was still shown and is described in John 3:16
We all have a choice, and if we live by God's Word
Righteousness will prevail and sin will seem absurd.

God is a gentleman and will not force us to do what is right,
But if you want to see change put down your weapons and get ready
for a spiritual fight,
Trust in the Lord and in the power of His might,
And I can ensure you that your true enemy, not humans, but the devil
will be put to flight.

The men looked up in amazement,
Then proceeded with conviction to make a statement,
"Oh how we were wrong for there is a God indeed!
In love He renewed our enslaved minds and now we believe!"

FUN FACT!

I had this idea where I was trying to create a conversation between some atheists and a Christian. This happens every day in our world but I would hope that more often than not the conversation ends like this one.

An encouragement to Christians out there:- it is not easy dealing with atheists, backsliders, and unsaved persons on a whole but do not give up, be Christ-like in all that you do, be compassionate and pray always. You do not need to always engage in everlasting debates, point out a few truths and leave it to marinate with them. They may not want to listen but one thing they do for sure is to watch the way you live your life, always looking for proof that you are a phony, or if you're truly a righteous saint. You will serve as their hope for proof that God is real; sometimes all they need is proof through someone else, and as ministers of the Gospel, Christ should always be known and presented through us ✟

IN A STILL SMALL VOICE

God: Come unto Me
Me: Wasn't I already there?
God: Come unto Me
Me: I didn't think I was far, I always felt near.

You're not listening beloved (God)

God: You need to draw nearer
Me: How much more?
God: Until you take on all my characteristics so much so that your character in me becomes clearer
Me: Hey, but I read your word so much that it takes residence at my heart's core.

God what do You really want? (Me)

God: I just want for you to listen to what I have to say
Me: I have been hearing You!
God: But not listening…there's a difference between the two…there's so much harm in you having
your own way
Me: Hmm…I thought just hearing You was enough, I really do.

SILENCE

Me: How can it be a bad thing that I wanna have my own way? What harm?
God: You keep going in circles like a windmill…I give you My peace but you have refused to be
still…and I keep telling you, the devil is seeking you to devour and kill.
Me: Ohhhh dear Lord…I can't fight this battle on my own! How do you expect me to remain calm?
How will I ever ride out this storm?
God: Depart not from under My covering,
There is no need for you to be anxiously hovering,
Peace be still, and abide in My will.
A prayer a day chases the devil away,
A fast per week puts the devil's plans to defeat,
The **Word** throughout the month reveals in your life My triumph,
Be ye ready, for this is the year that I the Lord may appear.

Me: Teach us Jesus Christ how to pray,
Lead us day by day as we strive to walk in Your way,
Raise up a generation who will war on their knees in prayer and fasting,
Thank You for Your grace and mercies which are from everlasting to everlasting.

FUN FACT!

I've got to let you know that this was my least favourite poem. I struggled with whether or not I should even include it in this book because of its stylistic difference. I think it is unique in its own way; it is a dialogue between God and a seemingly stubborn soul who wants to have his/her own way, and in reality this happens much of the time. As humans we fail to see the danger in us having our own way. Why can't we trust our Father who created us and promised us a hopeful future (Jeremiah 29:11)? He will not withhold anything good from us (Psalm 84:11).

EXTEND A LITTLE GRACE

What if…the next time you sin…
God doesn't choose to forgive?!
What will you do when you've lived your entire life…
…thinking that you're righteous,
But then get cast aside by Christ because you had the wrong motive?!

You see, Grace is God's unmerited favor to us…
We never deserved it, we were not a creation He could trust!
But out of the abundance of His love He showed mercy toward all of
us…
Yes ALL and not a fraction…
Grace was displayed as God's love in action ♥

This amazing grace was seen when God sent His son Jesus to bear our
iniquities
and die on that cross!
He sure showed the devil who's boss!
So the next time you encounter a brother who has wronged you, or
who has
faltered, before exercising vengeance or considering him a disgrace…
Remember where you are coming from and how Jesus has repaid you!
Remember to follow in His footsteps and extend a little…grace ♥

FUN FACT!

This is actually a spoken word! ♪ It is funny how when you are pushed to a corner that is when you discover some things about yourself, such as that you can write spoken words!!! But in truth and in fact many of us just aren't still enough to recognize ourselves (our gifts and abilities). Let this be an encouragement to you to take a sabbatical sometimes, listen to what God has to say and discover more about you ☺ Meditation is healthy, rest is vital. It is in the "be still" moment that you learn a lot! Trust me!

GOD UNDERSTANDS

God understands…
Every secret tear you cry,
All your seasons which feel so dry,
The many times you've failed no matter how hard you've tried,
The times you've refused to ask for help because of your pride.

God understands…
Every single thing about you,
The things which light your day versus the things which make you blue;
The many friends you have, you have an uncountable crew,
Yet when storms arise you can't even find a few.

God understands…
That you are perfectly imperfect,
But He never asked you to rely on anyone else's but His intellect;
The world won't always be kind to its subject,
But don't render evil for evil and become the devil's advocate.

God understands all things well,
He knows everything about you more than words can even tell;
So the next time you wonder, "Does God understand?"
Remember He formed you in the womb and He holds your destiny in
His hand…
So yes, He understands ☺

FUN FACT!

I am so very sorry right now for the people who are thinking that I am biased, prejudice, too righteous etc. because I have made almost all, if not all of my poems about God, but that's okay. Whatever you're going through right now, whatever is going on in your mind, God understands ☺ My relationship with God is an unbreakable bond for a reason. You see, He saved me, healed me, gave me peace, delivered me from hell; He makes me happy…the list goes on, I just can't say enough.

FROM GOD'S PERSPECTIVE

I look around and I see a broken world,
Sin sick souls that could make you hurl,
Tired bodies, sleepy eyes,
Sad husbands and trampled wives.

I've listened for a while…
Trying to make sense of what seems futile,
Busy bodied people, complaints and murmuring,
No one bothered to stop to pray they're too busy learning…

Learning?…yes, the ways of this life, their feelings and emotions,
Don't even get started about how much time it'll take from one's task
to have devotions…
It's traditional, it's history just like the pyramids,
It's a hindrance, a constraint, it is much like a salt grain that is acrid…

"I dare you to try me", says God Almighty,
I can give you peace in place of your worry and anxiety,
Just pause one day to give me a little of your time,
I promise you it won't be a waste, and to deny yourself this pleasure is a
serious crime.

FUN FACT!

When I was writing this poem I was really seeing from God's perspective the majority of souls who operated in this fashion. A small fraction of the world is "Christian", and out of that small fraction, a smaller fraction is really living a holy lifestyle. I couldn't help but to wonder how sad the Holy Spirit must really be feeling… I would feel frustrated. We get so busy being caught up in this world sometimes. At other times we just feel lazy to say 'hi' to God, and we fail to realize that we are indeed robbing ourselves of peace when we do not spend time with God; or, as far as I am concerned, it is a crime against our body (nature). That is the reason why I ended the last line the way I did.

STUCK IN THE PAST?

Aren't you tired of always looking back?
Imagining, that time would backtrack?
Is it something that you had lost?
Was it worth it? What did it cost?

The past is not somewhere to dwell,
It robs you of your freedom and cages you in a little cell,
From there there's not much you can attain,
Living like this, wow that's insane.

Enjoy this gift called the present,
It's a blessing from the Lord so be content,
Don't worry about past mistakes,
You're already forgiven, acceptance of this truth is all it takes.

Little is much when God is in it,
So keep going forward in faith and watch how you'll benefit,
The steps of the righteous are ordered by God,
It's time to put the past behind and lavish in the blessings that'll leave
you feeling awed.

FUN FACT!

This poem is for sure dedicated to my mother and everyone like her who needs to be healed from their past. One of the most paralyzing things in life is holding on to something that is already gone which consequently hinders you from moving forward. I do not know how many persons know that their emotional and spiritual well-being is also connected to their physical well-being, but it is. The mind is a powerful tool and whatever is conceived there can also spring forth into existence. For example, (this is a real testimony), when I was very young I wanted to become ill. I thought of being ill and wanted it (perhaps I didn't want to go to school the next day). All I know is that the very next day I was ill with the flu. There is also something called phantom illness (hypochondriasis) where persons worry so much about being ill that they become ill; this is just to show the connection between emotional and physical health.

Now, I am not sure if there are any scientific researches but unforgiveness can affect your physical wellness. All that bitterness and hatred can increase your likelihood of getting cancer, stroke, heart attack etc. This is known for sure amongst spiritual persons, but as I have said, I am not sure if scientists have dug into this interesting fact by linking unforgiveness to various diseases. However I am sure you can put two and two together and know that is true given that persons who are emotionally healthy are usually likely to live longer than persons who aren't.

HE MENDS THE BROKEN

Are you broken and torn up within?
Feeling as though you're not really living…
Jesus feels your pain,
For this cause He died and rose again.

Feel the weight of the world on your soul?
You're so burdened and feel so alone…
Jesus has been touched with your feelings,
Pour out your heart He'll do the necessary healings.

Drag yourself from one day to the next?
Hoping one day you'll find happiness…
Jesus will give you that joy,
He's a wonderful friend and ally.

Overwhelmed by the cares of the world?
Lost track of time and your vision gets blurred…
Jesus is the answer,
Trust Him with your life, He is the advancer.

FUN FACT!

This poem was inspired by a song by Elevation Worship "O come to the altar". I loved the song and the rhythm so much that I ended up writing a poem which conveys the message in the same way the song did. If sung, the same rhythm can be used as in the original song ☦

KEEP AT IT

They said you wouldn't make it,
But here you are, keep at it and be strong,
The world will always criticize you as they see it fit,
But remember who you are and never stay down for long.

They may look down on you,
Perhaps because of your past or your age or some other element,
Whatever it is never mind dear, keep your head held high and do the
best only you can do,
Don't let their eyes or words be an impediment.

They treated you unfairly,
And you cried night after night,
Yet you love so dearly,
As a result God will exalt you in their sight.

As you can see "they" will always find a way,
But the battle is not yours, it is the Lord's,
So straighten your crown son of God each day,
Never mind the world for you have awaiting for you your heavenly
rewards.

FUN FACT!

This wasn't for anyone specific, it was just an encouragement for those out there who are really going through it whether in the home, at school, at church or at the workplace; wherever you are, keep the faith and be strong and courageous, do not fear (Joshua 1 : 6, 7 & 9) for God is with you even unto the end of the world (Matthew 28:20).

THE STILL SKY

While the billows roll
And the storm clouds draw nigh
There is a hollow feeling in my soul
That cannot be quenched by any worldly high.

The sadness creeps in
There's no telling what is next
The darkness tries to win
But this unshakeable faith leaves the devil vexed.

Oh what a world
It is not always kind
Be careful for it'll leave your emotions in a swirl
There is a clear path that only the truly humble will find.

In the midst of everything
There is no question of what, when or why
For my destiny I am embracing
While I stand amazed looking at the still sky.

FUN FACT!

I kid you not, I don't know what got into me when I wrote this complicated poem (laugh out loud)! I was just sitting on my bed one night and words came to me and I just started jotting them down and lo and behold, it turned into a beautiful poem ☺

I GOT UP TODAY

I got up today in quite a contrary mood,
Didn't feel much like it but grabbed some spiritual food,
I realize each day is a fight,
And to win I've had to use all of my might.

I got up today, oh what a blessing it must be,
Not many are alive and well so it is a privilege to me,
I'm not always happy but I try to do my best,
Thank God for the strength so that in Him I can rest.

I got up today, took a deep breath and sighed,
Devil told me I'm not worth it, almost believed him then I remembered
all he's ever done is lied,
Had to brush it off and yes keep moving,
Onward to my purpose, why the devil he is still losing.

I got up today with the goal in mind to live fearlessly,
But I was still afraid so out of fear I threw away opportunities
carelessly,
But I will try again tomorrow and keep at it anyway,
I won't be discouraged because I knew it still took courage just to get
up today.

FUN FACT!

"I Got Up Today" marks the end of this inspirational poem series. This poem was for sure about me ☺ the fact that I got out of bed each day and fight to be the best me I can be is a blessing because it is not always easy. I've always struggled emotionally with being happy, with being at peace, and just living on a whole....so when I get up each day, trust me it's no easy task! It marks the start of a new battle I must fight each day (for family, relationships, job, peace, joy, the Fruit of the Spirit on a whole, my ministries and just about everything else).

I know I am not alone, so cheers to all you lovely people who are also doing your very best to get out of bed and fight for what you want legally and spiritually, even so on your knees in prayer and fasting. This poem is dedicated to you also.

With Love from Mischky

Mischka Reid is known for her motivational and jovial spirit among her peers and family members. She has a bachelor's degree from the University of the West Indies in Psychology (major), Management Studies (minor), and is currently pursuing her master's degree in Business Administration online at the University of South Wales. Ms. Reid considers herself to be a caring individual who works to encourage every soul that crosses her path. She hopes this is the first of many inspirational series to come. She lives with her family in Jamaica. You can reach out to her via email at

zabinda2k10@gmail.com

Made in the USA
Las Vegas, NV
13 March 2021